BY DEREK O'NEILL
Love/Divorce

Copyright © 2017 by Derek O'Neill

For information about permission to reproduce excerpts from this book write to:
Derek O'Neill
244 5th Avenue, Suite D-264
New York, NY 10001
E-Mail: info@derekoneill.com

ISBN: 978-1-936470-87-7
First Edition

All rights reserved, including the right to reproduce this work in any form whatsoever (audio, visual, electronic, etc.). Such reproduction is expressly forbidden without permission in writing from Derek O'Neill, except for brief passages in connection with a review. It is not the intent of the author to offer advice in any form, whether it is spiritual, psychological, medical, or other. If you are in need of special assistance or advice, please consult with a proper professional. The information within this book is offered as an avenue to inspiration and awareness. This book does not claim to possess all the answers, nor to heal or counsel. If you choose to apply the principles within this book to your life, that is your constitutional right.

Get a Grip Series © 2017
Editor: Nancy Moss
Front Cover Design: Derek O'Neill

DEDICATION

To all who read this book, I salute you for wanting to change the way you live for the better and for having the courage to be who you are as fully as possible.

To all who encourage me everyday to keep going and sharing their lives with me, family small and large. But most of all the little angels who came to teach me – Alexa and Blake, my grandchildren.

"Everybody hurts sometimes, and when we do it is nice to have Derek O'Neill around. His excellent little books on the things that get us, (fear, anger, depression, victimhood, mental blocks) allow us to find our way safely through our psychological minefields and arrive safely at the other side. Read them when you need them."

Paul Perry, Author of the
New York Times Bestseller
Evidence of the Afterlife

TABLE OF CONTENTS

Author's Preface..ix

Where We Begin, Where We End Up 1

Love Begins With You................................6

A Partnership Is More Than A Relationship..11

The Role Of Love 19

Divorce, An Unforeseen Reality 31

The Consciousness Of Love......................35

The Journey Of Divorce 39

After Divorce – A New Chapter................44

Meditation 48

About The Author..53

AUTHOR'S PREFACE

Thank you for purchasing *Love/Divorce: Soulmate or Cellmate?* This book has not come about as a result of my training as a therapist, but through some hard-earned lessons that I have experienced myself. This is how I know the path out of limiting beliefs and behaviors that hinder growth. The tools that I offer in this book have worked not only for me, but also for hundreds if not thousands of other people. I have shared these ideas and techniques in my workshops, one-on-one sessions, video and radio broadcasts, and on my website, and I have witnessed astounding results time and time again. Through observation of others, and myself, I have learned to identify the triggers and root causes of disharmony. Most of all, I have come to understand and apply the best methods for achieving peace and balance in life; not perfection, but real transformation and harmony that comes with learning who we are and what makes us tick. My 35 years of martial arts study has given me a refined sense of timing for when to strike with the sword to cut away old patterns, and when to use the brush to paint the picture of the life we deserve and can have.

The 'Get a Grip' series of books offers tangible, authentic wisdom that can help you in all aspects of your life. You've made a great choice by investing in this book. Enjoy the read, and take time to learn and apply the techniques. Let's change who we are together.

Derek

Love/Divorce
Soulmate or Cellmate?

WHERE WE BEGIN, WHERE WE END UP

No one can know where the journey that a couple takes together will lead. What keeps us together? What breaks us apart? Whether we remain in a romantic partnership, or transition out of it, there is wisdom in the idea of love driving both experiences. It is too easy to see marriage/partnership in "success" or "failure" terms. It's much more productive and healing to look at the dynamics of love and divorce with new eyes. Let's redefine the journey we take with another person, no matter how long it lasts.

If you are in a relationship, working on keeping what brought you together alive and adaptable, or at some stage of divorce (heading into it, in process, or dealing with post-divorce life), it is helpful to understand that your experience is about YOU. Yes, a partnership is about two people – but your power in love, life, joy or in crisis, and in resolution rests with your own being. Your self-love and confidence, even when shaken, remain under your control. Whatever you are going through, I want you to realize and believe in your true power. Stop giving it away. Don't put people on pedestals who don't belong there and don't let someone else dictate your happiness. We can go through challenging and/or painful times with a partner but no one sets the tone of your life except you. You are every bit as powerful as anyone else on this planet.

Love and partnership can lift us up, but the danger is that once these feelings change, they are now tied to your identity. In a relationship, or out of one, remember that self-love is the main ingredient in the recipe of being at peace with the world. There will be highs and lows in every aspect of your life. When a marriage ends, it can be one of the most difficult experiences along your path. There's no sugarcoating it, yet the very thing that brought you into the partnership can be the thing that brings you out, with as much healing as possible. You will have the opportunity to gain a strong sense of who you are, independent of anyone else. This core concept will help you in relationships that last 50 years, ones that fall apart in a relatively short time, and every manifestation in-between. Life is a journey into the highest and most powerful part of yourself, your heart. Partnerships allow us to share this with someone else. They also test our hearts when they come undone. Love can set the tone throughout the entire journey.

My marriage to my late wife Linda was about two beings coming together and supporting one another no matter what we had to face, no matter where we were in our journey. I like to think of us as a couple who were looking in the same direction in life, with the intention to follow the same path, yet as separate souls who were not dependent on the other person to make us complete. We never stifled our individual growth. Though Linda was called back to the light in 2008, she is always with me. She continues to be my teacher as she was in life, now even more so. A marriage/partnership is always changing. Linda taught me, and reinforced the idea that we had to sustain the balance of what it means to be "together" in a healthy, realistic way that never takes away from the "self." When it comes to endings, we can transition into our new situation with the knowledge that we have experienced life head-on, instead of sitting on the sidelines never taking a risk. Sharing our love is an act of courage that can shed light on everything we do.

On the pages that follow, we will look at the role of love – for others and for ourselves – in partnerships. The first section looks at some of the issues that can create challenges, and the second part of the book focuses on the journey coming out of a marriage/partnership and the post-divorce/break-up experience when we re-establish who we are, what we want in life and how we can act on and share what we have learned.

LOVE BEGINS WITH YOU

It is hard to have a satisfying partnership if your ego is out of alignment with love. What do I mean by that? As you sit with yourself, your feelings, your past experiences, and your self-image, it is common to want to deflect, avoid or ignore the things that cause us fear, lack of confidence and a feeling of being incomplete. When you push away the part of your ego you'd rather not deal with, it is very hard to feel self-love and acceptance. If we come to a relationship thinking we can align our ego "separate" from our partner, rather than "with" our partner, we are running from our shadows, which will manifest in disharmony. You must embrace who you are before you can enter a partnership. That's not about being what you perceive as "perfect" or "issue-free." It's knowing that when two people get together they bring their baggage with them. Unpacking it is what a relationship is going to be about. You cannot hide the contents from your partner, and even more importantly, yourself. You also can't dump the contents of your baggage at the feet of your loved one and expect them to deal with it. You must be willing to unpack, work at, and accept the issues that you will have together and individually.

How does your partner feel about themselves? Obviously, we are all unique and have different experiences at any given time, yet if a couple has a wide divide when it comes to self-acceptance and love, it will show up in the relationship as imbalance. When we acknowledge that we must love ourselves in order to love another, that's a conscious commitment that becomes a very important part of a partnership. If your spouse/partner does not have that kind of emphasis on self-love, it can cause many issues and conflicts. There's an exercise I have people do where they rate how much they love themselves on a scale of 1-10. Again, we are not all the same, and just because someone is grappling with feelings doesn't mean that a relationship cannot be strong, but how your partner sees themselves on that scale can predict problems.

Just as you face the ups and downs of a relationship – hopefully together – another much less talked about element, is how you feel about yourselves. A strong partnership will recognize that as something that must be active and evolving. No matter what you go through as a couple, if one of you begins to try to fill an emptiness, or avoid deep-seated issues by expecting the other person to "fix it," it is almost always a guarantee of trouble.

Accepting love is something you can only truly do when you know that you are perfect as you are. There is almost always work to be done, but you are meant to be exactly where you are at any given point. Surrender to the fact that there are things you cannot control and outcomes are never guaranteed. Your journey is your destination. In a partnership or marriage, we make conscious decisions – at the beginning in terms of who we choose, and throughout the relationship with every event and situation we face. However, forcing and reaching for certainty will only lead to suffering. You must be willing to accept love, in all of its inexactness and different manifestations. When it comes to a marriage, that may mean having to go your separate ways. Most people's biggest fear is of being loved. When a loving human crosses your path, you should be ready to surrender your fear and feelings of self-doubt. If you bring them into the relationship, the push and pull of love will be difficult. If you begin with knowledge of your worth, your heart, and your ability to project the love you have found for yourself, however imperfect, you will have a great advantage in a true and sustained partnership.

Marriage and partnership may be versions of "togetherness" but it's the attention and time that we spend on ourselves (and *just* for ourselves on a regular basis) that will ward off feelings of abandonment. Fear of love is tied to fear of abandonment. You must start by not abandoning yourself. If you don't, you'll unconsciously push away your loved ones and you feel the very thing you are trying to avoid – abandoned. Sit with yourself. Begin to love yourself warts and all. Though we don't hear this enough, self-love – and your partner's self-love – are the seeds for a good marriage.

A PARTNERSHIP IS MORE THAN A RELATIONSHIP

When we marry, or enter long-term partnerships, we are setting out to work with someone else towards shared goals. Before this kind of commitment is made, a relationship tests the support, sharing, harmony (or lack of) and the chemistry (physical and emotional) between us. The shift to this new definition can be jarring for a couple, but until you start down that pathway in your life together it's very hard to know just what it will be like. Intimacy, consideration, and common ground in a relationship certainly form the bedrock for marriage. Yet a formal bond creates a distinctive "us" that will now function alongside your individuality, navigating both daily and future situations, making decisions, facing challenges, experiencing joy, celebration, and sorrow. If you have children, another dimension of your relationship opens, again changing the landscape of what it means to be a partner and presenting a journey that has its own peaks and pitfalls.

One of the most basic concepts for a partnership to work is the idea of the impermanence of everything. This is true even in a marriage that lasts 80 years! We are constantly changing, as is our spouse. Life is constantly changing on its own. Your partnership is either going to ride those waves of change, or not. It will need to adjust. It will need to take a step aside at times, or it will become more reactive. We tend to delude ourselves into thinking that love will be enough. Sometimes what feels like love can be more of a projection of our ideals instead of reality. There's a fine line between the trust we put in love and the delusion we are susceptible to. Does the love between you and your partner accept one another for who you both are, or are one or both of you projecting what you want in each other, rather than what you *have* in the partnership? Can you go down the road of cooperation, shared goals, and commitment to facing life in its unpredictable nature, together?

Love is active. Love is mindful. A marriage/partnership makes that even more abundantly true. Two beings joined together are never stagnant together or apart. That's one of the reasons marriage is hard. You are each traveling on your own, and as a couple. Marriage is about being apart as much as it is about being together. You must be able to adjust, modify and repair to keep the union healthy and strong. The members of a partnership take care of themselves and one another. This is key. One side of this doesn't work without the other.

Happiness always comes from within, whether you are in a partnership or not. A marriage where one or both people in it look to the other to fill that happiness is destined for trouble. When a relationship makes you happy, it's easy to fall into the trap of feeling that happiness is tied to your partner. They are not the source, rather it's the feelings that you each bring to the union that creates happiness. If you don't have access to your own happiness, you can't create the kind of emotional foundation to weather the ebb and flow of a long-term relationship. It's no wonder that not all marriages can survive; it is a tricky balance to maintain the "self" element of a partnership while giving of yourself freely, without the greed or egotism that puts expectations on the other person. In a marriage, we should rely on one another, but also be independent. We should share but not give ourselves away. We should grow but not compete. We should be vulnerable but not fragile. You don't have to come to a partnership with these elements working seamlessly; rather it's the commitment to be aware, and work on them that makes a union.

There is no marriage/partnership that doesn't evolve – whether positively or negatively. Romance plays a big role in the beginning of a relationship. Even in the most loving marriages/partnerships, the passion that you start with is going to change. It does not have to go away, it can in fact strengthen, but it is going to change. The focus that you put on one another is also going to vary over the course of time. Sometimes out of necessity because of situations, and sometimes just naturally, based on the journey your life takes. Having children certainly reinvents the dynamic between a couple. Starting a family can solidify a relationship, but it can also begin a process of unraveling if a couple are not willing to adjust to the new landscape of their union and work at keeping the partnership cared for and healthy.

Marriages are always in flux and nothing remains "new" and "fresh" unless you go from one person to the next, never sustaining a true interpersonal connection and commitment. In a long-term relationship, the curtain is pulled back. Our lives now include the other person's feelings and experiences, no matter how grounded we may be in a strong sense of self. The union creates a whole new set of ups and downs, not just the ones we go through individually. The challenges are great. We are going to experience perhaps more pain and hurdles than we would have alone, yet the benefits of a partnership are abundant. The human need for community/family is beautifully symbolized when two people make a commitment to one another. When we support, share, create, care, and allow ourselves to love and be loved, we are reaching for our highest state of being.

Remaining mindful throughout a partnership is one of the most important goals. Even if your marriage dissolves, we can approach ANY experience with awareness and contemplation to ease our journey. There are many valid reasons why we end relationships. We may find that we do not have enough in common. Perhaps we never did, or the way we have changed as an individual has made sharing our lives together unworkable. Maybe communication has broken down in a way that cannot be repaired. What is most important is that the things that brought you together before hold their place in your life as being valid at the time, and need to be cherished as part of your story. A marriage that survives difficulties must go back to the core of what joined you in commitment to your significant other to begin with. A divorce can't always be harmonious, but we can still honor the role of love in our lives. When it changes, it might turn our world upside down initially, but if we don't abandon the idea of loving fearlessly, we will find our new path and thrive.

THE ROLE OF LOVE

It can be helpful to look at the feelings and emotions that surround marriage/partnership through the lens of love. If we see love – whether it is the fear of it, the struggle of it, the joy of it – as a connective thread, it can define our relationships, even when they end.

LOVE VS. DESIRE

Desire can be a component of love, but it should never be confused with *being* in love. When a couple joins together, chances are that the physical and chemical desire is strong and compelling. But what can desire, in the bigger definition of the word, bring about that can cause issues between people? The problem with desire is that it sets up expectations and can cloud our judgment. It can leave us feeling that something is missing if the physical or emotional aspect of a relationship ebbs and flows, or we don't possess the object (in this case a partner) of our desire in the way we imagined we wanted. Desire – the kind that grasps or forces – causes suffering and we can see that played out in marriages. A partnership between people must be actively worked on but at the same time there's an acceptance of where you are and who you (and your partner) are, in the moment. If you are fighting this it can only lead to disharmony. You are where you are supposed to be and you will always get what you need in perfect timing.

Being critical of your partner, even if not in spoken form to them, is a manifestation of the desire to change someone. This is one of the most problematic elements in a marriage. The only one who can change anything about themselves is that person.

When we share a life with someone it is all too easy to begin to desire that certain things are different. We can distract ourselves from taking care of ourselves, maybe even obsessing about "if only" something was not happening or he/she would stop a behavior. We are trained from an early age to think about how things "should" be. When we bring this line of thinking into a marriage/partnership, we will only be disappointed and suffer. The only "should" is to shift desire when it arises to a greater mindfulness, and service to a higher power or God. When you stop desiring for yourself, you can be present in all of life, and in this case, the union of your partnership.

ADDICTION TO LOVE

Love, by its very nature, can be an addicting force in our lives. Our goal is to have love be at the core of all we do and experience, yet when we need it to fill an emptiness or play out a scenario we imagine we must have to thrive, we are twisting the role of love and its meaning in a relationship. Our past can trigger an unhealthy connection to what we have come to see as love, even though it may be a negative reinforcement. If we were made to feel that we were unlovable, it can create a desperation to find what we think we need to validate us. How many times have we heard about people marrying someone just like their cruel or abusive parent? Perhaps you can see that in your own life. It's clear that people who have been hurt by someone that was supposed to love and care for them, such as a parent, often go looking to capture that love from a spouse who reminds them – usually subconsciously – of the parent whose love they desperately wanted. It is a pattern that can become an addiction. It can manifest in the case of someone whose parent showered them with attention and what felt like overwhelming love, when as an adult, that person seeks out unrealistic adoration from a partner. In both cases, and in all the other versions of what we bring to the table of a marriage, we must look at our past to inform who we are and what we need to work on before it becomes a recurring problem in our lives.

ANGER AND FEAR

Unfortunately, anger and fear can stand in the way of love in a partnership. All emotion is energy and when we are angry we are reflecting a hurt and/or fearful mindset outwards. When we turn the energy inwards, it manifests as depression. People make partnership commitments to others without understanding how fear is steering the ship. How does this look? Maybe you've made a commitment to a long-term partnership but you are fearful of losing yourself in the relationship, or you have been hurt by someone in your past. You could inadvertently be pushing your loved one away to avoid the pain that you subconsciously fear is on the way. Misplaced anger creates a toxic environment for true love to grow. On the flipside, anger projected inward, causing depression, sets a tone in a partnership that is stressful and challenging.

Situations can arise from the relationship that bring about anger, but what if we stop ourselves before the anger is projected towards our partner, recognize it, look at where it might be coming from, then deal with it appropriately? This is self-care that is also caring towards your partner. Internal aggression causes far more damage than external aggression ever will. It is a mirror of the inner suffering. You must be focused and disciplined to bring peace to your heart. This is something that couples can work on individually, and together. It's all about tolerance – for yourself, your feelings, your past, and for all those elements in your partner. A marriage is like two streams that are running alongside each other. The water will flow if the streams are not blocked or contaminated. They are going to the same place but each have their own nature. Resistance, in the form of anger and fear, will affect the journey you are on with your partner.

The way that we treat ourselves is critical. If your relationship is not working, you must deal with it, whether it survives or not. The issues behind the trouble are rarely just the result of what goes on between you and your partner. Everything that's happening to you right now has not come to hurt you, but to wake you up. If you play the victim role it will keep growing and causing problems, no matter who you are with (or if you are single.) Victim consciousness is going to keep you from fully living. You need to find a way of looking at what the real issues are.

Anger is a mirror. When there's anger in a relationship, that's you. When you can practice self-love, a new mirror appears that can transform you and the way you relate to your partner. If you try to fool the mind without removing the energy, the energy is just going to pop back up again. You must remove the energy in order for healing to take place. Emotions put issues in place for us and it takes emotion to remove them. Emotion is the lid that keeps everything repressed in you. If you don't have the knowledge and tools to deal with those feelings, they are going to create a negative script that runs through your mind (which affects your partnership.) All emotion, happiness and sadness included, comes from inside of you. No one "makes" you feel what you are feeling. Both love and anger show up as a chemical reaction. If you have taken the effort to practice being a loving person, you can begin to let go of negative emotion. The idea of practice is important, for patterns – both positive or negative – reinforce themselves. Anger creates more anger. Peace manifests more peace.

Fear stands for "False Evidence Appearing Real." You may go through an entire relationship fearing that you are going to lose it. This is not love. Love is not giving over your power to someone to make you happy or sad. The way to push against this and come back to the truth of love is to be present, and live in the "now." Experience what you are feeling and own those feelings. They don't come from someone else or anything that begins with them. Love is sitting with the present, not fixated on a past that is gone and a future that has not arrived. Your fears come to you so that you can embrace them with love and compassion. We do lose relationships and we do lose people but compassionate detachment, embodied in the nature of love, is the only path to true healing.

ATTACHMENT, DETACHMENT AND COMPASSION

A successful partnership based on love has the inherent nature of attachment, yet must always have detachment as a simultaneous thread running throughout. Couples who support one another can easily fall into a co-dependent pattern. Healthy love has healthy detachment. We know where we start and stop in relation to our partner. We know what we are responsible for and what we are not. You have to recognize attachment before you can practice detachment. We cannot deny attachment to everything; our partners, family, friends, jobs, or our bodies. You must acknowledge it all to reach a consciousness where you are willing to let go of dependence on any of it. That doesn't mean that you do not give and receive love, enjoying all the gifts that life offers, nor do you stop feeling the effects of challenges and disappointments.

To feel nothing or go numb is not detachment. Detachment is not counting on anything staying the same because it can all change at any given moment. A stable relationship is not truly stable, if we define "stable" as meaning inert. When you accept the pendulum of life swinging back and forth, you are approaching the kind of detachment that makes living as a loving being possible. You can feel the pain of others without stepping into the melodrama surrounding or suppressing it. Attachment is when you believe that you need something and you won't be able to live without it. This will lead to problems in a lasting partnership, and even in one that ends. Your life, moving forward, must hand attachment over to God or a higher power. Suffering will manifest when we don't stay on the path we were given to experience. When you see God in everything, you will understand the beauty of the world.

Compassion is an important part of partnership/marriage but detachment is part of compassion. Without detachment, we can end up hurting those we mean to help. Love should come without strings or conditions. To love without need is to offer compassion. It is what I call ordinary love, not based on what you get from someone else or what you expect. Whatever a partnership gives you – years of happiness, children, challenges and perhaps over time, change that makes it impossible to stay together – you have been offered life lessons that you can welcome with open arms and compassion for yourself and your partner. Whatever you have manifested in your life, you have for a reason, and you can un-manifest it as well, your choice. All you need are the words "I AM" to change a negative to a positive…I am healthy, I am happy, I am compassionate, etc.

DIVORCE, AN UNFORESEEN REALITY

Ending a marriage or long-term partnership can be one of the greatest challenges we face. It is often likened to a kind of death. No one enters a marriage planning for its demise. We all know that a substantial number of marriages don't work out, and that some couples who remain together are not happy. If we are divorced we may look at "successful" marriages and think that was unattainable because of something lacking in us, or in our choices. As we look more closely at the experience of divorce, and all of its complications, let's take out judgment or comparison. In the previous sections of this book I've highlighted some issues that may lead to a partnership ending, but no one is immune to having to a major shift in some aspect of their life and having to adjust. Again, everything is changing, always, and every experience is valid and valuable. If your marriage ended you have not failed. You have lived. Open your mind to a new way of looking at what you see as mistakes or regrets. Divorce is a highly emotional and intense experience. There are ways to journey through it that can make it easier, yet sometimes we have no control over circumstances that arise. There can be anger, jealousy, fighting, custody and/or financial issues. Even a divorce that seems "easy" isn't usually as simple as we'd like. Often feelings are delayed. It's uncommon to just skip away and go along your merry way!

Part of the disruption of divorce can stem from the shift from being on the same team, so to speak, to now being on different sides of the table. This person you loved and cared for enough to embark on a life together now exists in your life in a whole new context. If the decision to split up was mutual it can ease some of the complexities, but your identity as a partnered person into a single person is still going to need attention and self-care. You could be feeling any combination of fear, resentment, anger, shame, or abandonment. These emotions, when under the umbrella of divorce, have a heighted sense of urgency at first. Divorce is a legal process but the emotional process is much greater. How can we move through the experience with the least amount of pain and disruption? How can we turn the page in our life and start anew? How can you, if possible, find a resolution with an ex that is not toxic and damaging? What role does love – now redefined – play in your divorce? The love between you and an ex will change, and in many cases entirely, but you can go through the experience as a *loving being*.

Divorce can have you feeling very alone, not just in the separation from your partner, but from the world. You may know many others who have been down this road but when you are fresh into the process it can be extremely isolating. One of the most important things I can say is to seek out support, whether that be a close friend or family member who is available to you emotionally, a group, or a therapist/counselor. A split can involve so many elements, we may feel there's no time for self-care, but it is now more important than ever. Get enough sleep, eat as well as you can, meditate, and try to exercise, even if it's a short walk. Remember to breathe! What may feel like a very dark time will change over time. You will find that the difficulties you go through will begin to lighten, and though this is hard to see when you first split up, ending a partnership can be a tremendous opportunity for growth. It will be a time that you learn about yourself. Perhaps more than you ever would have in the marriage/partnership, especially one that was impossible to stay in.

THE CONSCIOUSNESS OF LOVE

The love you felt for a partner may fade, or be disrupted by hurt, but to acknowledge that you married for love (I'm assuming you did!) can keep you consciously aware of the bigger concept of approaching divorce as a loving being. You can also acknowledge the pain as a loving being. If you have both made the decision to end the marriage, keeping the heart open toward a shared goal, albeit one you had not expected when you got together, can help on the path to healing. If only one of you wants to end the partnership there will be a different, more difficult dynamic, yet there's the opportunity in that experience to practice teachings that will help with every step along the way. Compassion may be the last thing you are feeling for your spouse, but when we are cognizant that the compassion is also beneficial for you, it becomes a goal to reach, even though it will take time. Time and divorce are intertwined. You will move from feeling to feeling, not necessarily in a straight trajectory. There will be good days and bad. You will take two steps forward, then maybe one back. But overall, you will grow stronger and wiser, especially if you never lose your connection to love. That connection will be tested but it's up to you to remain mindful to a deeper love all around you.

You will need to let go of attachments to what you thought things were going to be like in your life. We all make plans. Our society seems to revolve around projecting our future, but so much of it is an illusion. You control your inner life, but we cannot know what is in store for us out in the world. And when a marriage ends, as shattering as it can feel, that emptiness creates a space to fill. Before you can move forward and be available for whatever is meant to come your way, you must sit with that empty space. Embracing and accepting your pain is not wallowing in it; rather it's letting go of outcomes, not clinging to the past or future.

Mindfulness can be a challenge once the wheels of separation start turning and you are plunged into a series of steps toward a new life. The present can feel unpleasant and scary. Being attentive and aware of what's going on around you and what you are feeling can keep you grounded and alleviate some of the stress. Mindfulness breaks down our experiences and makes them less daunting. No matter the circumstances of your breakup, you will need to move through it one step at a time. You may know where you want to go – or where you have to go – in your new identity as a single person, but becoming overwhelmed is going to paralyze you. The feelings are raw, judgment is impaired, and emotional triggers are all around you. This is the time, as are other severely unsettling times (such as the death of a loved one), where staying conscious of love, and the healing power of love in service to others, is essential.

THE JOURNEY OF DIVORCE

One or both of you have come to a decision to split up. Your world feels upended, even when the divorce was something you wanted. Do not avoid your feelings, whatever they are and however they arise. To do so only creates more suffering. There will be many things to take care of, both physically (living arrangements, money issues, children's visitation, etc.) and emotionally. Try to achieve a balance between doing what you need to do and not becoming overwhelmed. You have been part of a couple but you are still who you are, even in your new context. Society tends to label people and categorize them. We hear the phrase "marital bliss" (an overblown idea – no marriage is always blissful!) and think that is the goal that is expected of us.

You must work against the idea that you are less than, or have failed at something. Ultimately your divorce might very well be one of the most positive transitions that you can go through.

To love someone does not mean you are necessarily going to stay together. Love doesn't say that the changes you experience as an individual will nonetheless keep you on the same page as your partner. Love is not enough when it comes to shared lives. Love does not have to include romance, which might have waned. Love wants you to live your life to its fullest. The respect a divorcing couple can have for one another is to believe that concept and embrace it as they part. Though the anger that can arise when you go through a breakup – and the fighting that sometimes ensues – can set the tone initially, love is there in a new form. Be mindful of it. If you are, you become more resilient to the challenges that lie ahead as you go through the process. Try to operate from a place of love, not hurt or fear of the future.

Splitting up can be an expression of love. You are opening your life to have more happiness by not staying in a relationship you are no longer meant to be in. In time, you might be able to experience a new connection to your ex as a friend, though this isn't always possible or necessary. If you have children, you are still going to be a family. There is a whole set of feelings and arrangements that are going to have to be dealt with, but the best approach overall, is to remember to put your children first and know that co-parenting is going to have to be worked on, always. If your kids are old enough, talk honestly to them about the transition. Remind them that love for them, and for the family, is unwavering and the most important thing for all of you. Don't talk negatively about your ex with your children. When people embark on that, it can be extremely destructive. You may be hurting terribly from the split, but you must be as adult, steady and supportive to your children as humanly possible.

It's important to keep perspective while going through a divorce. Emotions will be high, but try to continue to connect to the world and spend at least some time focusing on what counts to you, outside of being part of a couple. Now is a great time to practice gratitude. Make a list, take a daily inventory, and always be mindful of what is beautiful and joyful in your life and in the world. If you have children with your ex, find the ability to appreciate that the marriage has brought you this amazing source of love and light. Love created your family, even if the situation is going to change. Whether it happens early in the process of divorce, or only after a stretch of time when the healing is slower, thanking an ex for what you *had* with them can be extremely helpful for closure. You need to realize that expressing this gratitude is for you more than for anyone else. It will lift resentment and anger, which you are probably turning back on to yourself. Allow truth and kindness – toward yourself and others – to guide you.

AFTER DIVORCE – A NEW CHAPTER

Suffering arises from wishing that your life had gone down a different path. If we look at reality, your life is *always* on course to be different. We cannot recapture what is gone, and by spending energy on replaying the past or imagining what "would have been," you are standing in the way of the potential for growth and happiness. The universe doesn't deliver all our lessons at once. There are speed bumps! When you are in divine timing, everything exists for a reason. There is no "slow" or "fast," only "what is." The new chapter in your life that will begin after a divorce may not feel like a welcome one, but you have the power to approach it as an opportunity.

Adjusting to your life after the end of a marriage/partnership is different for each person but it rarely all falls magically into place. There will be a period that feels unsettling. Remind yourself that this is perfectly normal. If you have children, they are adapting to all the changes. You will be focusing on them, but don't forget to take care of yourself. Friends and family may be giving you advice or encouraging you to go out. Support is wonderful but you need to listen to your own needs. Take your time. Many people will try to compensate for whatever they are feeling. Some will jump into new relationships quickly, looking for validation of their being attractive and lovable. Know that the validation must come from within. Getting to a place of strong self-love may take a while. Allow this process to unfold. Be mindful of your decisions and actions when you are fresh out of a marriage. You may be much more susceptible to your triggers. Try to act with intention, not react to emotion.

Learning to love again might mean learning to trust again – this is a process. It is important to connect with your feelings, accept them, but also not allow them to take on a life of their own. You might be grappling with insecurity, or shame, or fear. Your financial situation may have been affected. If you are sharing custody of children, you are adjusting to periods of not being with them. All of this can affect how you feel about love. It would be easy to become convinced that you cannot open your heart again. Divorce can be a crossroad where you must consciously make the decision to know that you can love, maybe not today or even tomorrow, but at some point. When you have healed and gained perspective, you will be able to ask yourself "What do I want?" and "What do I need?" Maybe you never truly sat with these questions before. Now is your chance.

After a divorce, think about your growth. What have you learned? You have loved another person and even though you are no longer together, you take that ability to love back out into the world. Can you help others and be of service because of your experience? Life is a series of beginnings and endings, for everyone. All of us live in a cycle of events and situations that make us human. We have the capacity to be loving beings as we move through our time here on earth. No matter what brings you to this point in your life, know that you are not alone and you have so much to offer to the world when you tap into the love that resides within you!

MEDITATION

Whether you are trying to nurture the love in a challenging marriage, going through the stages of divorce, or coping with long-term healing after a breakup, meditation can play an incredibly helpful role. Meditations and exercises that address stress and provide relaxation techniques are particularly beneficial. Here we combine awareness of your body in the present, letting go of tension, and concentrating on love – no matter how many contrary feelings come up – to use as a guidepost for your journey through difficult times.

Find a quiet, peaceful setting and 10-15 minutes that you are free of any task or expectation. Even 5 minutes is worthwhile. If there's a lot of chaos going on in your life, and you think you don't have time to meditate, remember that is one of the very reasons it's important to do it! Your mind is probably very busy, and your body is at a heightened state of anxiety. Make an announcement to your mind and body that it is time for a pause.

Sit in a comfortable position, either on the floor or a chair. Close your eyes. Keep your back straight and think of a string coming up from your spine, holding your head tall. Take three deep breaths, inhaling through your nose and exhaling through your mouth. Continue to breathe slowly and deeply, with awareness.

Starting with your feet, feel the energy that exists inside and around them. Release any tension you are feeling there. Once your feet are relaxed, slowly move up your body and focus on each part – your shins, your knees, your thighs, your stomach/torso, up to your chest, neck, and head, up to the top. Feel all the energy that flows through your body, along with the energy around it.

Now bring your concentration back to your chest and settle it in your heart. Visualize the energy as the love that resides inside of you. Sit with that feeling. Introduce, in your mind, the person or situation that you are struggling to see in a loving light. It can be your spouse/ex. It might be a financial situation or child custody complication that is causing negative or dark feelings. It could be an upcoming event, such as a visit to a lawyer or a conversation with your partner/ex that you are hesitant about.

Continue to visualize the person or situation, then come back to your heart where you have cultivated a loving light. Send that light out to the person or problem. It may be difficult to feel what you perceive as love in that moment, but think of love as energy and light. It is there to help you most of all. The love that you surround a person or situation with, that is causing you anxiety, is self-love that can become compassion even in the most adversarial of dynamics. If you are experiencing hurt and/or anger, that can make this meditation seem very challenging. Acknowledge what you feel, then let it go, if only for a few minutes. Know that time will change and heal feelings, in whatever way it is meant to be. Project to the future where there will be more peace of mind.

Sit with the mind of love, clear of other emotions, for the rest of your meditation. If thoughts or feelings come up, greet them and then envelope them in the light. When you are ready to end your meditation, bring your concentration back to your breath and open your eyes.

Along with sitting meditations like the one above, mindful meditation, which you can practice as you go about your day, keeps you focused on the present and on your feelings. When we are mindful of our surroundings and feelings, we are better able to cope with trials and tribulations.

Remember – take care of yourself! Exercising, eating healthy food/regular meals, and getting plenty of sleep are all so important during stressful times. Please seek out counseling or therapy if you feel overwhelmed, along with friends who love you and can be supportive. Though marriage issues, divorce/breakups, and adjustment to being single can feel very isolating, know that you are truly not alone. Above all, be kind, compassionate, and patient with yourself.

ABOUT THE AUTHOR

For more than 30 years, Derek O'Neill has been transforming the lives of thousands of people around the world for the better. An internationally acclaimed transformational therapist, motivational speaker, author, martial arts sensei and humanitarian, Derek inspires and uplifts people from all walks of life through his workshops, consultations, speaking engagements, media, and tireless humanitarian work.

Drawing on thirty years of training in martial arts, which earned him the level of Master Black Belt, coupled with his extraordinary intuitive abilities and expertise as a psychotherapist, Derek has pioneered a new psychology, transformational therapy. His signature process, aptly named "The Sword and the Brush," helps clients to seamlessly transmute their struggles into positive outcomes, using the sword to cut away old patterns and the brush to help paint the picture of the new life that they require.

In addition to reaching large audiences through workshops and media, Derek advises individuals, celebrities, business leaders, and politicians, helping them to find new perspectives on long-standing issues and bringing harmony back to their lives and businesses.

Author of More Truth Will Set You Free, the Get a Grip series of pocket books, a cutting edge book on parenting titled Calm Mama,

Happy Baby, and several children's books, Derek also hosted his own radio show, "The Way With Derek O'Neill," which enjoyed the most successful launch in VoiceAmerica's history, quickly garnering 100,000 listeners.

Derek is a master at offering practical wisdom and proven techniques for living a more harmonious and fulfilling life, bringing CEOs to the level of wise yogi and wise yogis to CEO; he has worked with executives from some of the world's major airlines, and the cast of Spiderman on Broadway to help transform group disharmony and untapped creative potential into productivity and dynamic performance. He has been featured in Exceptional People Magazine, The Irish Independent, The Irish Examiner, CBS television, and RTE, Ireland's national TV network.

Inspired by his worldly travels, he formed SQ Foundation, a not-for-profit organization focused on helping to solve global issues facing humanity today. In 2012, he was honored as Humanitarian of the Year and named International Celebrity Ambassador for Variety International the Children's Charity. He was welcomed as Vice President of the esteemed charity in May 2013.

Recordings of Derek's discourses are available for download, offering practical wisdom and proven techniques for living a more harmonious and fulfilling life.

MORE RESOURCES FROM DEREK O'NEILL

Get a Grip Book Series
Abundance: Starts Right Now
Addiction: What a Cover-Up!
Anger: Who Gives a Shite?
Bullying: You Won't Beat Me
Confidence: Easy For You to Say
Depression: What's that?
Dreams: The Best Messengers
Excellence: You Never Lost It, You Forgot It
Fear: A Powerful Illusion
Forgiveness: So I Can Move On
Gratitude: Yes Please
Grief: Mind Boggling But Natural
Happiness: You Must Be Effin' Joking!
Love/Divorce: Soulmate or Cellmate?
Mindfulness: Out Of Or In Your Mind?
Relationships: Would You Want to Date You?
Stress: Is Stress Stressing You Out?
Suicide: Fast or Slow
Weight: What's Eating You?

Other Books
More Truth Will Set You Free
Calm Mama, Happy Baby

Children's Books
Water Drop Coloring Book
The Adventures of Lucinda in Love-Filled Fairyland

SOCIAL MEDIA
YouTube
youtube.com/DerekONeill101
Facebook
facebook.com/DerekONeill101
Twitter
twitter.com/DerekONeill101
LinkedIn
linkedin.com/in/DerekONeill101

www.ingramcontent.com/pod-product-compliance
Lightning Source LLC
Chambersburg PA
CBHW071541080526
44588CB00011B/1749